SCHIRMER'S LIBRARY
OF MUSICAL CLASSICS

Vol. 1545

G. F. HANDEL

Six Sonatas

For Violin and Piano

Edited by

ADOLFO BETTI

G. SCHIRMER, *Inc.*

DISTRIBUTED BY

HAL•LEONARD®
CORPORATION

7777 W. BLUEMOUND RD. P.O. BOX 13819 MILWAUKEE, WI 53213

G. F. HANDEL[1]

Born in 1685, at Halle. Handel began at a very early age to give unmistakable signs of musical genius. When he was but 11 years old, his performances and improvisations on the organ were already remarkable. After completing his musical education. and studying law at the University of his native town, he went to Hamburg, where, from 1704 to 1707, he was at first violinist and later harpsichordist in the opera-house. During this period he wrote several operas and an oratorio. Then, on the invitation of Gian Gastone, of the Medicis, he visited Italy, writing operas and oratorios as well as numerous compositions in smaller forms, both vocal and instrumental. His opera *Agrippina*, performed in Venice in 1708, was especially successful. In 1710 he went to London where, with *Rinaldo*, he achieved a triumph never equalled by any previous work of the kind in England. From 1712 on he lived almost uninterruptedly in or near London.

For more than half of the years that he spent in England he was chiefly a composer of operas (he wrote 36 of them); then he gradually turned his creative activity towards the oratorio, which brought him immortal fame. In 1742 he wrote (in 23 days!) the *Messiah*, first performed in Dublin. Several other oratorios followed, with varying degrees of success. But his old age was on the whole serene and comfortable, in spite of the blindness that afflicted his last years.

He died in 1759 and was buried in Westminster Abbey.

* * *

Handel's complete works, as published by the "*Händel-Gesellschaft*," comprise 97 volumes. Of these the twenty-seventh is devoted to the "*Kammer-Sonaten*" (Sonate da Camera). There are 36 of them: 21 for various combinations of instruments (2 violins, or flutes, or oboes), and 15 for a solo instrument with harpsichord.

The Violin-Sonatas belong to this last set, which was first published about 1724. Although showing here and there influences from Italy (Corelli) and from England (Purcell), they are on the whole typically Handelian, in both style and inspiration.

As the student will not fail to remark, in most of the slow movements the melodic line is exceedingly simple and bare. To us to-day they seem the more eloquent for this simplicity. But apparently such was not the opinion of the listener in Handel's time. For in those days the custom was for the performer, probably in order to show his virtuosity, to improvise ornaments ("graces") on the melodic scheme provided by the composer. This practice, already in use in the time of Corelli (1653-1713), was maintained all through the eighteenth century up to and including Viotti (1753-1824)—whether with the approval or the tolerance of the composers themselves is still a matter of debate among musicologists.

At any rate, in order that the student may become acquainted with a practice that has now gone completely out of use, a *Double* (an embellished version) has been provided for the Largo of the Sonata in E major (No. 6), after the manner of the period.

A. B.

[1]The spelling adopted here is the one that the composer used in his later years. In the MSS. of the Italian period (1706-1710) we sometimes find "Hendel," which is closer to the original German "Händel," but afterwards this entirely disappears.

CONTENTS

86858

Sonata I

3rd of the 15 Sonate da Camera, Händel-Gesellschaft Edition, Volume XXVII

Edited by Adolfo Betti

G. F. Handel
(1685-1759)

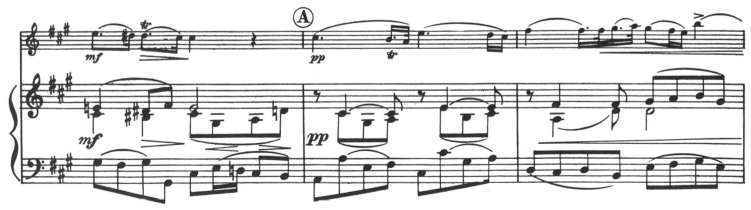

Allegro (non troppo) ♩. = 96

Sonata II

10th of the 15 Sonate da Camera, Händel-Gesellschaft Edition, Volume XXVII

Allegro (con brio) ♩=120-126

Adagio ♩ = 66

mf espressivo

mf (la 2da volta sempre **p**)

mf

p

2da volta poco ritenuto

mf (la 2da volta come sopra)

p

Allegretto ♩. circa 104

f

sf > p

poco a poco

f

p

poco a poco

cresc.

f

p

f

cresc.

mf

p

f

p

cresc.

p

cresc.

Sonata III

12th of the 15 Sonate da Camera, Händel Gesellschaft Edition, Volume XXVII

Adagio (ma non tanto) ♩ circa 56

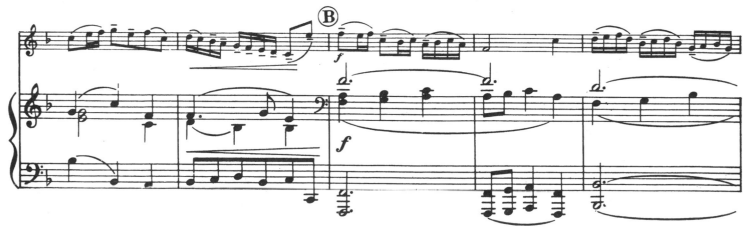

Allegro (assai vivace) ♩=144

Violin

SCHIRMER'S LIBRARY
OF MUSICAL CLASSICS

Vol. 1545

G. F. HANDEL

Six Sonatas

For Violin and Piano

Edited by

ADOLFO BETTI

G. SCHIRMER, Inc.

DISTRIBUTED BY

HAL•LEONARD®
CORPORATION

7777 W. BLUEMOUND RD. P.O. BOX 13819 MILWAUKEE, WI 53213

G. F. HANDEL[1]

Born in 1685, at Halle, Handel began at a very early age to give unmistakable signs of musical genius. When he was but 11 years old, his performances and improvisations on the organ were already remarkable. After completing his musical education, and studying law at the University of his native town, he went to Hamburg, where, from 1704 to 1707, he was at first violinist and later harpsichordist in the opera-house. During this period he wrote several operas and an oratorio. Then, on the invitation of Gian Gastone, of the Medicis, he visited Italy, writing operas and oratorios as well as numerous compositions in smaller forms, both vocal and instrumental. His opera *Agrippina*, performed in Venice in 1708, was especially successful. In 1710 he went to London where, with *Rinaldo*, he achieved a triumph never equalled by any previous work of the kind in England. From 1712 on he lived almost uninterruptedly in or near London.

For more than half of the years that he spent in England he was chiefly a composer of operas (he wrote 36 of them); then he gradually turned his creative activity towards the oratorio, which brought him immortal fame. In 1742 he wrote (in 23 days!) the *Messiah*, first performed in Dublin. Several other oratorios followed, with varying degrees of success. But his old age was on the whole serene and comfortable, in spite of the blindness that afflicted his last years.

He died in 1759 and was buried in Westminster Abbey.

* * *

Handel's complete works, as published by the "*Händel-Gesellschaft*," comprise 97 volumes. Of these the twenty-seventh is devoted to the "*Kammer-Sonaten*" (Sonate da Camera). There are 36 of them: 21 for various combinations of instruments (2 violins, or flutes, or oboes), and 15 for a solo instrument with harpsichord.

The Violin-Sonatas belong to this last set, which was first published about 1724. Although showing here and there influences from Italy (Corelli) and from England (Purcell), they are on the whole typically Handelian, in both style and inspiration.

As the student will not fail to remark, in most of the slow movements the melodic line is exceedingly simple and bare. To us to-day they seem the more eloquent for this simplicity. But apparently such was not the opinion of the listener in Handel's time. For in those days the custom was for the performer, probably in order to show his virtuosity, to improvise ornaments ("graces") on the melodic scheme provided by the composer. This practice, already in use in the time of Corelli (1653-1713), was maintained all through the eighteenth century up to and including Viotti (1753-1824)—whether with the approval or the tolerance of the composers themselves is still a matter of debate among musicologists.

At any rate, in order that the student may become acquainted with a practice that has now gone completely out of use, a *Double* (an embellished version) has been provided for the Largo of the Sonata in E major (No. 6), after the manner of the period.

A. B.

---

[1]The spelling adopted here is the one that the composer used in his later years. In the MSS. of the Italian period (1706-1710) we sometimes find "Hendel," which is closer to the original German "Händel," but afterwards this entirely disappears.

CONTENTS

86858

Sonata I

3rd of the 15 Sonate da Camera, Händel-Gesellschaft Edition. Volume XXVII

Violin

Edited by Adolfo Betti

G. F. Handel
(1685-1759)

Violin

Sonata II

10th of the 15 Sonate da Camera, Händel-Gesellschaft Edition, Volume XXVIJ

Andante (con gravità) ♪ circa 80

mf espressivo

Violin

Violin

Sonata III

12th of the 15 Sonate da Camera, Händel-Gesellschaft Edition, Volume XXVII

Adagio (ma non tanto) ♩ circa 56

Sonata IV

13th of the 15 Sonate da Camera, Händel-Gesellschaft Edition, Volume XXVII

Violin

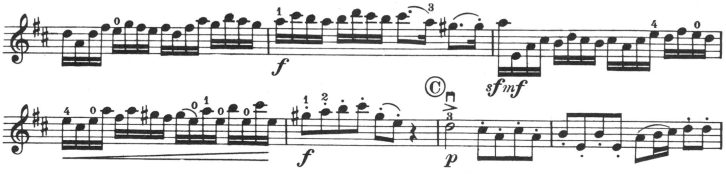

36358

Violin

Violin
Sonata V

14th of the 15 Sonate da Camera, Händel-Gesellschaft Edition, Volume XXVII

Violin

86358

20

Sonata VI

15th of the 15 Sonate da Camera, Händel-Gesellschaft Edition, Volume XXVII

Violin

Violin

Violin

Sonata IV

13th of the 15 Sonate da Camera, Händel-Gesellschaft Edition, Volume XXVII

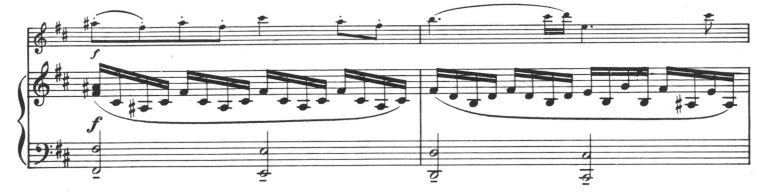

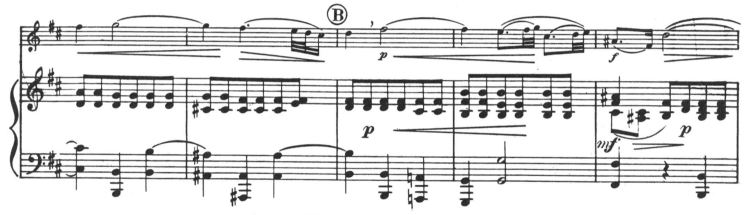

Allegro (con brio) ♩ circa 188

Sonata V

14th of the 15 Sonate da Camera, Händel-Gesellschaft Edition, Volume XXVII

Allegro (moderato) ♩=96-100

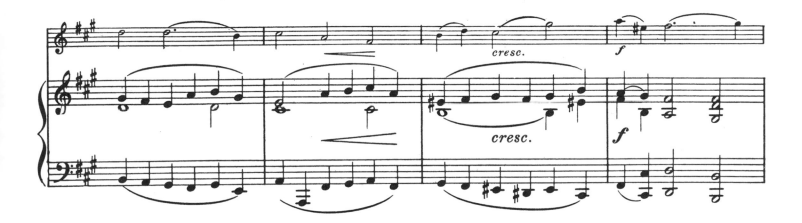

Allegro ♪ = 160 - 168

Sonata VI

15th of the 15 Sonate da Camera, Händel-Gesellschaft Edition, Volume XXVII

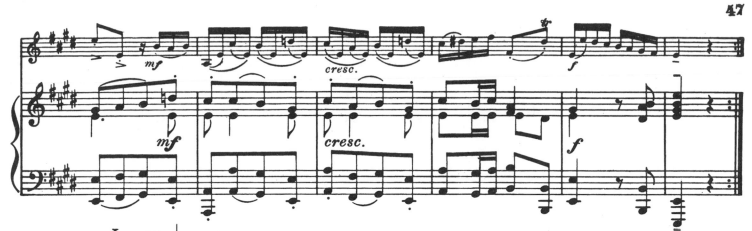

Largo ♩ = 88-90

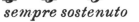

Largo (Double)

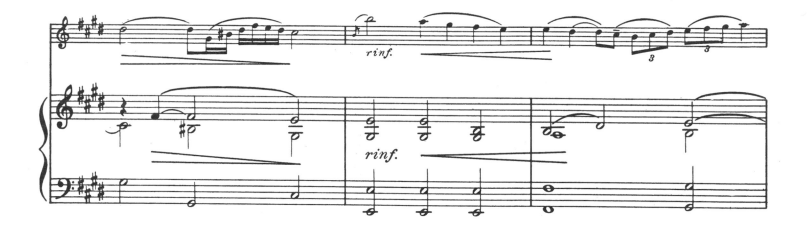